FOOTBALL LEGENDS

Troy Aikman

Terry Bradshaw

Jim Brown

Dan Marino

Joe Montana

Joe Namath

Walter Payton

Jerry Rice

Barry Sanders

Deion Sanders

Emmitt Smith

Steve Young

CHELSEA HOUSE PUBLISHERS

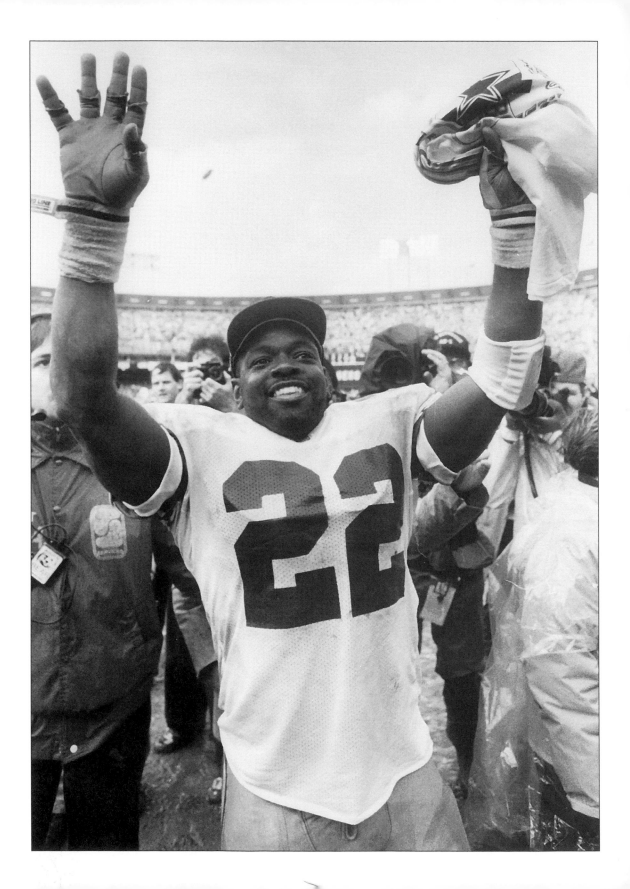

FOOTBALL LEGENDS

EMMITT SMITH

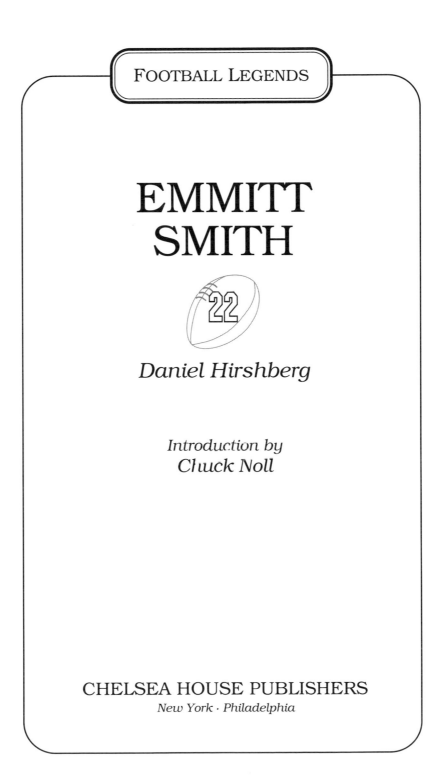

Daniel Hirshberg

Introduction by
Chuck Noll

CHELSEA HOUSE PUBLISHERS
New York · Philadelphia

Produced by Daniel Bial and Associates
New York, New York

Picture research by Alan Gottlieb
Cover illustration by Bill Vann

3 5 7 9 8 6 4

Hirshberg, Dan.
    Emmitt Smith / by Dan Hirshberg.
    p. cm. – (Football legends)
    Includes bibliographical references and index.
    Summary: Traces the life of this football player from his
childhood in a Florida government housing project to his being a
star for the Dallas Cowboys.
    ISBN 0-7910-2461-X
    1. Smith, Emmitt, 1969- ¬Juvenile literature. 2. Football
players–United States–Biography¬Juvenile literature. [1. Smith,
Emmitt, 1969- . 2. Football players. 3. Afro-Americans-
-Biography.] I. Title. II. Series.
GV939.S635H57 1996   95-22881
796.332'092–DC20   CIP
    [B]   AC

CONTENTS

A WINNING ATTITUDE

Chuck Noll

Don't ever fall into the trap of believing, "I could never do that. And I won't even try—I don't want to embarrass myself." After all, most top athletes had no idea what they could accomplish when they were young. A secret to the success of every star quarterback and sure-handed receiver is that they tried. If they had not tried, if they had not persevered, they would never have discovered how far they could go and how much they could achieve.

You can learn about trying hard and overcoming challenges by being a sports fan. Or you can take part in organized sports at any level, in any capacity. The student messenger at my high school is now president of a university. A reserve ballplayer who got very little playing time in high school now owns a very successful business. Both of them benefited by the lesson of perseverance that sports offers. The main point is that you don't have to be a Hall of Fame athlete to reap the benefits of participating in sports.

In math class, I learned that the whole is equal to the sum of its parts. But that is not always the case when you are dealing with people. Sports has taught me that the whole is either greater than or less than the sum of its parts, depending on how well the parts work together. And how the parts work together depends on how they really understand the concept of teamwork.

Most people believe that teamwork is a fifty-fifty proposition. But true teamwork is seldom, if ever, fifty-fifty. Teamwork is *whatever it takes to get the job done*. There is no time for the measurement of contributions, no time for anything but concentrating on your job.

One year, my Pittsburgh Steelers were playing the Houston Oilers in the Astrodome late in the season, with the division championship on the line. Our offensive line was hard hit by the flu, our starting quarterback was out with an injury, and we were having difficulty making a first down. There was tremendous pressure on our defense to perform well—and they rose to the occasion. If the players on the defensive unit had been measuring their contribution against the offense's contribution, they would have given up and gone home. Instead, with a "whatever it takes" attitude, they increased their level of concentration and performance, forced turnovers, and got the ball into field goal range for our offense. Thanks to our defense's winning attitude, we came away with a victory.

Believing in doing whatever it takes to get the job done is what separates a successful person from someone who is not as successful. Nobody can give you this winning outlook; you have to develop it. And I know from experience that it can be learned and developed on the playing field.

My favorite people on the football field have always been offensive linemen and defensive backs. I say this because it takes special people to perform well in jobs in which there is little public recognition when they are doing things right but are thrust into the spotlight as soon as they make a mistake. That is exactly what happens to a lineman whose man sacks the quarterback or a defensive back who lets his receiver catch a touchdown pass. They know the importance of being part of a group that believes in teamwork and does not point fingers at one another.

Sports can be a learning situation as much as it can be fun. And that's why I say, "Get involved. Participate."

CHUCK NOLL, the Pittsburgh Steelers head coach from 1969–91, led his team to four Super Bowl victories—the most by any coach. Widely respected as an innovator on both offense and defense, Noll was inducted into the Pro Football Hall of Fame in 1993.

1

GET IT TO EMMITT

It was not looking very good for the defending Super Bowl champions, the Dallas Cowboys. In 1993, just one year earlier, the Cowboys had crushed the Buffalo Bills in the championship game, 52–17. Now, in Super Bowl XXVIII, the same two teams were facing off, and the first half belonged to the American Conference title-holders. This was the Bills' fourth straight trip to the Super Bowl—a record—but they were still looking for their first win. When the two teams went into the locker room at the half, the Bills were feeling good about themselves, holding a 13–6 lead.

During the break, a frustrated Emmitt Smith, Dallas's outstanding halfback, turned to offensive coordinator Norv Turner and said, "Get the ball to me. It doesn't matter how, just get it to me."

And that's just what Turner did.

Smith had missed the first two games of the

Emmitt Smith stretches as he looks forward to the Super Bowl.

This fourth-quarter touchdown helped the Cowboys win their second consecutive Super Bowl over the Buffalo Bills, 30–13.

regular season because of a contract dispute, yet amazingly he still won the rushing title that year—for the third straight time. He had dislocated his shoulder in the regular season finale a few weeks earlier, but in the next game he still managed to rush for 168 yards on 32 carries to lift the Cowboys to a thrilling 16–13 overtime victory over the New York Giants that gave them the NFC title. The National Football League has a number of star running backs—the Bills' Thurman Thomas has to be counted in that number—but Emmitt Smith is widely regarded as the best.

The Cowboys tied the game up early in the third quarter when James Washington returned a Thurman Thomas fumble 46 yards for a score.

From there on it was the Emmitt Smith Show.

When Leon Lett forced Thurman Thomas to fumble, James Washington scooped up the ball and ran for the touchdown. This set the stage for a sensational Cowboy—and Emmitt Smith— comeback.

The Cowboys stopped the Bills cold on Buffalo's next possession, and on the Cowboys' next offensive series, both Turner and head coach Jimmy Johnson turned to Smith. It was imperative at this point to establish the run. With the often-injured quarterback Troy Aikman having trouble moving the ball through the air (Aikman would finish with 19 of 27 completions for 207 yards), the ground game would need to pick up. Smith answered the call, and in a hurry.

The league's most valuable player became the Cowboys workhorse, running seven of the next eight plays and gaining 61 of 64 yards to bring Dallas down to the Buffalo 18 yardline. Smith wrote in his autobiography: "Now I'm coming back to the huddle screaming. Screaming to my teammates on the sideline, screaming to my teammates in the huddle, screaming so loud I'm sure the Bills can hear me, but right now I really don't care. I'm screaming, 'Yeah! This is what I'm talking about! This is what I'm talking about! Give it to me again! Give it to me again!'"

Smith finally sat a play out, then returned on the next play and with 8:42 remaining in the stanza, blasted his way 15 yards for a touchdown on one of many "power right" (or as it is sometimes named, "counter trey") calls during the drive. At 5'9", 210 pounds, Smith is the prototype of a great runner. He goes from standing still to running at top speed very quickly, and his top speed means very few people can keep up with him. His strength allows him to run over tacklers, but he can spin and cut his way around tacklers too. A huge advantage is his vision. "When I line up, I don't see the wide receivers or the cornerbacks, but I see everybody else," he says. "It's a clear picture." This allows him to find holes and alleys to run through that other backs might miss.

On the opening play of the final quarter, Washington, who was having a sensational day himself (he finished with a game-high 11 solo tackles), intercepted a Jim Kelly pass. The Cowboys quickly marched down to the 6 yard-line, and Smith was called on three straight times to run the ball. He got the ball down to the 1, but Buffalo's defense prevented the touchdown.

Many coaches, on fourth down, would have been happy to go for the easy field goal. But Jimmy Johnson had no intention of doing that. Emmitt took a pitch from quarterback Troy Aikman and slammed his way into the end zone to put the game away.

"I knew Emmitt would find a seam on the pitch and he did," said Jimmy Johnson.

An Eddie Murray field goal finished the 24–0 second-half scoring. The Cowboys won, 30–13, earning their second consecutive Super Bowl title.

Smith's final stats for the day were scintillating. He finished with 132 yards on 30 carries. He also caught four passes for 26 more yards. His counterpart on the Bills gained a paltry 37 yards and fumbled twice, including the one that resulted in Washington's TD return.

Smith's numbers seem even more amazing when one realizes that he was playing with a shoulder still sore from the Giants game. "It bothered me," he admitted. "I got hit on it a couple of times and a guy fell on me. In a big game like this, though, you've got to learn to play with it. I did not want to come out because of the shoulder." Bum shoulder aside, he thus became, along with Miami Dolphin full-back Larry Csonka, the only runner to rush for more than 100 yards twice in a Super Bowl game.

He also broke a Cowboys team record by gaining over 100 yards in post-season play for the fifth time, and it marked the 100th 100-yard game of his football career, including high school, college, and pro. He added the game's Most Valuable Player award to his post-season resume, making him the first runner to win a rushing title, a regular season MVP crown, and a Super Bowl MVP crown. Afterward, teammate Michael Irvin said simply, "Emmitt played Emmitt's game."

"Being MVP of the league and this game, too, you can't ask for anything more," Smith said in the postgame press conference, minutes after leaving the field with his goddaughter, Kendra, in his arms. "I started out missing the first two ball-games and got hurt in the mid-part of the season and was behind everybody in rushing. I was able to capture that and get back in and help the team win. It's been a great, great season for the team and myself. This was the final piece in the puzzle. I could not ask for anything more."

The game's most valuable player makes sure he does not fumble the Super Bowl trophy.

2

GOLDEN CHILD

Shortly after Emmitt Smith turned nine years old, his life changed in a big way. Up until that year, Emmitt had played quarterback on his midget football team. It was the dream position for every kid his age. But suddenly, his new coach told him that from now on, "You're going to run the ball for us." Within a week, Smith, already bursting at the seams with muscles, felt right at home.

This would be his second year of organized football, although there were scores of games played in backyards, in sandlots, and in parks before then. The oldest son of Emmitt, Jr., and Mary Smith, young Emmitt also had an older sister, Marsha, and three younger brothers—Erik, Emory, and Emil.

Emmitt displayed unusual signs of strength and mobility at an early age. Mary recalls the time she and her husband were watching TV when Emmitt—only nine months old—crawled

At Escambia High School, Emmitt helped turn a poor football team into a state champion.

up to them. "Just a little baby, and already he could climb out of his crib," she exclaimed.

Emmitt's early football prowess did not thrill his father. Luckily, his mother supported him from day one. It would not be until Emmitt had been playing a few years before Emmitt, Jr., would agree that football suited his son just fine.

For Emmitt's first eight years, the Smiths, a close-knit religious family, lived in a government project in Pensacola, Florida. His father drove a bus for a living, but with five kids money was often tight. Like other projects around the country, violence was a fact of life, with gunshots sometimes ringing out in the calm of night and robberies and fights happening all too often. Drugs, too, were commonplace. So was the sight of monster-sized rats. Yet the Smith family always tried to make the best of a rough situation.

Finally, by the time Emmitt was nine, the Smiths were able to move out of the projects. Emmitt's next home was a house behind where his grandparents lived, several blocks, yet several light years, away from the projects.

Emmitt's first football team was the Salvation Army. He was big for his age throughout his "midget career," with opposing coaches many times questioning Smith's true numbers at weigh-ins. Later on, Smith would actually have to *lose* weight in order to play in games. And as he grew, his weight forced him to play with older kids. While he held his own during those games, it was a challenge every time out.

Once he made the move to running back, it all came naturally for Smith. He found that his vision of the action on the field was improved and the extra few yards he had to accelerate after getting the handoff gave him another advantage. Playing quarterback soon became a nonissue for Smith. The weight issue continued to haunt him, though, when Smith, 13 at the time, became ineligible to play a year of football. The midget league cutoff was 160 pounds and Emmitt was already up to 180 pounds. Instead of taking the handoff, Smith spent the season instructing other running backs what to do with the ball when they took the handoff.

Weight problems would be a thing of the past the next year, however. Smith graduated from Brownsville Middle School and started attending nearby Escambia High School. Dwight Thomas, Escambia's new coach, remembers the spring day when he first met Smith, then in eighth grade. "I'm over at the middle school and as you can imagine with eighth graders, it was just wild," he says. "Here walks up to me this really well presentable young man. He's wearing nice clothes, nice shoes. He's like a young adult. I mean he weighed about 180. I thought he was 18 or 19 the way he presented himself. He comes up to me and says, 'Hi, I'm Emmitt Smith.' "

Smith proceeded to tell Thomas that he wanted to play football. Thomas found it hard to believe that Smith was for real. "I wanted to check his transcripts," he admits.

Thomas had heard about Smith, but then again, he had heard about a lot of other "midget greats" over the years. It did not take long for Thomas to realize that Smith was indeed the real thing. "The first week of drills I knew he had great athletic ability. He wasn't even in pads yet, but I could tell real, real quick." It was

Smith rushed for over 100 yards in each of his last 28 high school games. Here he goes off for a big gain against Northeast High.

at this point that Smith decided to devote himself fully to football. He gave up organized basketball in the winter (he was a pretty good hoopster, leading Brownsville to a city championship in seventh grade and another fine season in eighth grade), and followed a regimen for the next four years that had him lifting weights during the winter for strength and running track in the spring to add to his speed.

In the fall of his freshman year, Smith was a starter in the backfield for a team that had wallowed in despair for many years. In 18 years,

Escambia had just one winning season. It was coming off a one-win nine-loss season and a three-year record of 3-27. Escambia had a reputation as one of the worst teams in the state. In a word, it stunk. But Thomas, who was fired from his previous job because they told him he could not bring his team to the next level (despite a four-year record of 30-12), and Smith both felt they had something to prove.

Smith made his point right away, during his first game. Playing predominately with sophomores (Thomas had cut 26 seniors), Smith rushed for 115 yards and scored two touchdowns. Later in the season, Smith had games of 205 and 210 yards en route to a 1,000-yard year. Escambia finished the campaign at 7-3 with Smith a key ingredient. According to Thomas, the team tied for the district championship.

The next two seasons were even better for Smith and Escambia. His sophomore year the team went 12-2 in earning Florida's 3-A championship, beating a much bigger Bartow High School in the title contest. Another state crown followed the next fall. This time, Escambia claimed the 4-A title, which includes the state's largest schools, thus making the championship the most prestigious of them all. Smith gained over 2,000 yards, seven times eclipsing the 200-yard mark in a game. The Gators were too much for the heralded defense of Bradenton South in the championship game, winning by three touchdowns. Smith gained over 150 yards and was a thorn in South's side all day.

Emmitt became aware of his unusual visual powers in high school. During some games, he had the field so well mapped out in his mind that "I'd run to the hole with my eyes closed."

By the time Smith's senior season got under-way, Escambia was ranked number one in the country. The team—and Smith—was a sought-after story. ESPN, *Sports Illustrated, USA Today* and several other national publications were finding their way to the northwest strip of Florida. Everything was going Escambia's way as it headed into a major showdown with its crosstown rival, Pensacola High.

Escambia led early, 10–3, and it looked as if the Gators would run away with the game when Smith broke free for a 51-yard touchdown in the third quarter. But the refs said Smith went out of bounds. The touchdown was nullifed. It was the break Pensacola was waiting for, and it came back to win, 17–10.

Thomas remembers Smith's and his squad's reaction afterward. "For two hours he wouldn't take off his helmet," says the coach. "Nobody did. There was a lot of crying in the locker room."

As it turned out, that loss cost the Gators a playoff spot even though they were 9-1 at the end of the season. So Smith and his teammates played the string out with their hearts, finishing with another successful campaign but no cham-pionship.

In his four years of high school ball, Smith put up some of the greatest numbers ever, any-where. He rushed for 8,804 yards, averaging 7.8 yards per carry. He gained more than 100 yards in 45 of the 49 games he played. Amazingly, he went over the century mark in each of his last 28 games. In addition, he scored 106 touch-downs. *Parade Magazine* declared him the best high school football player in the country.

"In 30 years of coaching I've never had any-one as mentally tough as him," insists Thomas, who most recently coached Godby High School in Tallahassee. "I've been around a lot of great players but he was definitely the toughest one mentally and physically. You could injure him, but you could not hurt him. I think he's that way because of his parents. They are very sup-portive of him. A lot of kids can't reach out because they are searching to find who they are. But Emmitt did not have to do that. He knew where he came from so he could concentrate 100 percent on football. God gave him a lot of ability and his parents gave him the rest."

Indeed, Smith was held in high regard not only on the football field but in the classroom. He was in the top 100 in his class. Yet when it came to football, he took it a step further. He never missed a practice, and in fact, was never late for practice or a team meeting. "This is a kid who was goal-oriented," says Thomas. "I never had to discipline him, never had to go after him."

The colleges, on the other hand, chased after Smith like he was gold.

3
GATOR TIMES

They came from all over, the college recruiters, to the Smith home in Pensacola. They came at all hours, and they called even more frequently as decision time neared. It had started during Emmitt's sophomore year, first with letters. "Hello, don't forget us when it comes time to decide on a college," the letters said. In his junior year, it got a little more intense and by his senior year, Smith was inundated with letters, phone calls, and visits.

Just about every major college in the country was seeking his services; all were offering scholarships. Among the coaches who visited the Smith household were Auburn University's Pat Dye and Florida State University's Bobby Bowden. It eventually came down to a handful of schools, with Auburn, the University of Nebraska, and the University of Florida as the front-runners.

Helped in good part by his mother's recom-

Mary Smith helped Emmitt decide that he would attend the University of Florida. He is shown here announcing that decision.

Future teammate James Washington (number 3) cannot catch up with Emmitt Smith at the 1987 Aloha Bowl.

mendation, Emmitt finally decided on Florida. In Gainesville, they had struck gold.

"By the time Emmitt was a sophomore in high school he was a legend in the state," notes John Humenki, Florida's sports information director. "When he came here it was like a legend was coming and that's the way the media played it."

At the football team's annual Media Day that first summer in 1987, Smith was the center of attention. Swarms of reporters surrounded him.

Only the team's quarterback, Kerwin Bell, attracted as much attention.

Florida was coming off of probation, but that did not bother Smith. After all, he had joined a high school football team that had been mired in losing ways for years. He had met that challenge and here was another.

The year before, the Gator rushing game averaged a paltry 3.3 yards a carry. That, plus the fact that the program was rebuilding, marked a good opportunity for him to play as a freshman, he thought. Coach Galen Hall said as much. So did the media, labeling him the "savior" before he even ran the ball once. "I feel bad about all this attention," he told reporters back then. "Freshmen shouldn't be getting all this (attention). Seniors should be the ones sitting in the middle of all this attention. They are the ones who are going to lead this team. Not me."

Emmitt did get to play a lot as a freshman, and he made quite an impact. He was played sparingly in the first two games, but in his first start, he carried the ball 39 times for 224 yards—a school record. Ever after, he was a prime figure in the Gator offense.

Emmitt went over 100 yards in eight games that year—including six games in a row. Four times he rushed for over 170 yards. Emmitt averaged almost six yards per carry and finished the season with 1,341 yards—the most in the Southeastern Conference. He was the first freshman since Herschel Walker of the University of Georgia to lead the SEC in rushing as a freshman. He surpassed the 1,000-yard mark in only his seventh college game, earlier than any other player in college football history. Indeed, he became only the second freshman to finish in the top 10 voting for the Heisman Trophy. (Tim Brown, the University of Notre Dame wide receiver, was named the best college player that year in a controversial vote.)

Despite Emmitt's success, the Gators did not have a particularly good year. The popular Kerwin Bell led them at quarterback, but otherwise Florida had few marquee players and finished the campaign at 6-5, losing three of their last four games, including a 20–16 decision to UCLA in the Aloha Bowl. Ironically, Smith played against several future Cowboys teammates in that game, with the Bruins featuring the likes of Troy Aikman, James Washington, Ken Norton, Jr., and Frank Cornish. For the rookie back, though, it was a spirited campaign.

Smith's sophomore season brought more problems. New offensive coordinator Lynn Amedee brought in a pass-oriented offense. Suddenly, Smith was no longer the go-to guy, at least not like he was used to. The star back could not argue at the start, though, since the Gators won their first five games handily, with Smith gaining over 100 yards in each contest. In the fourth game of the season, in fact, Smith reeled off a 96-yard touchdown run, the longest in school history.

But in the sixth game, versus Memphis State University, the team's fortunes started to change. For the first time in his life, Emmitt was seriously injured. A strained ligament is not a dangerous condition, but it was painful and serious enough to keep Smith out of action for over a month.

Smith did not take the news very well. "The next few weeks were stressful and depressing," he admits in his autobiography. Rather than dwell on the injury, Smith jumped into his schoolwork even harder and began rehabilitation in earnest.

The Gators lost the Memphis State game, and they lost two of the three games in which Smith had to watch from the sidelines. (They also had a bye week.) Emmitt did not start in the next game—a loss to Georgia—but at least he got to play.

Smith then rushed for 113 yards in a win over the University of Kentucky. In the last game of the regular season, Smith was held to 56 yards by arch-rival Florida State in a 52–17 setback that gave the Gators another mediocre 6-5 record. Still, they got a bid to the All-American Bowl, where they beat the University of Illinois and their star quarterback Jeff George, 14–10. Smith rushed for 159 yards and scored 2 touchdowns.

Even before Smith's junior year had started, rumors began to surface that he would be forgoing his senior year at Florida. He scoffed at them at the time, preferring to deal with the task at hand—playing football for the Gators. Of course, it was not that easy. Again the Gators had a new offensive coordinator, Whitey Jordan.

In Jordan, Smith found a coach he agreed with and the combination triggered several big games for the tailback. Florida lost the opener to the University of Mississippi but rebounded with four consecutive wins over Louisiana Tech, Memphis State, Mississippi State, and LSU.

Five games into the season, another dramatic event took place. Galen Hall stepped down as head coach; Gary Darnell took over the reins. The team was stunned. Why would Hall quit in the middle of a promising season?

In Darnell's debut, Smith gained over 100 yards in the first half and finished with 202 as Florida ripped Vanderbilt University, 34–11. Up next was the University of New Mexico, and Smith had one of his best games ever. He racked up an incredible 316 yards on the ground, including 3 touchdowns. He was en route to 1,599 rushing yards for the season—yet another school record for Emmitt.

After a win over Kentucky, Florida went into its annual late-season skid, with losses to Auburn, Georgia, and Florida State. In three years at Florida, Smith never tasted victory over any of those SEC powers. In the Freedom Bowl, the Gators were blasted by the University of Washington. Smith was held to a career-low 17 yards.

Even with his subpar outing against Washington, on the surface, all looked terrific with Smith following the bowl game. He led the team in rushing (breaking the school record in the process), averaged almost 150 yards a game, was selected the SEC Player of the Year, was a consensus first-team All-American choice, and finished seventh in the Heisman Trophy voting. He claimed he was not looking to turn pro.

In a hurry, his tune changed and with good reason. It was announced not long after the season that Steve Spurrier, a former Florida standout, was coming back to coach the team. Darnell and the rest of the coaching staff were out.

For Smith, this meant a third new head coach and a fourth offensive coordinator. How excited could he get about learning yet another system, and hoping the coach would appreciate his skills?

Finally, on January 31, 1990, Smith made an announcement. He was entering the NFL draft.

"Emmitt had been through a tough three years," says Humenik. "We were not real successful as a team. We were not really in contention for conference championships and we were not in the picture for big bowl games. Obviously everyone would have loved for him to stay but you could not really blame him. He had gone through three offensive coordinators and two head coaches. You felt for him. As it turned out once everyone saw Steve Spurrier's system you realize you have given anything to see Emmitt play in it. In his three years here he was a tremendously marked man. Even though he gained a lot of yardage, we did not have a system to take that pressure off him. Under Spurrier, he would not have had to rush 30 times every game. Defenses would not have been able to line up 10 or 11 guys on the line and dare him to get by. The feeling here was that we did not get to see him display his full talents."

Not see his full talents? In three years, the three-time All-Southeastern Conference back had gained 3,928 yards and established 58 team records.

Interestingly, in Spurrier's first season, the Gators went 9-2 and had a share of first place in the SEC. By then, Smith was making big bucks in the NFL.

4

A STAR ON THE HELMET

When the draft came in April of 1990, the rumor mill had Emmitt going to teams like the Seattle Seahawks or Tampa Bay Buccaneers. The Cowboys' first pick was the 21st and he was sure he would be gone by then. The Cowboys had sent a scout to watch him work out a couple of months earlier, but that was the last he had heard of it. On draft day in New York, meanwhile, football executives were drooling over an especially strong crop of athletes.

As usual, the Sunday morning draft was broadcast live by ESPN, and all around the country college players hoping to make it to the big show were anxiously watching the tube. Jeff George was the first chosen, taken by the Indianapolis Colts; next, running back Blair Thomas got the call from the New York Jets. Cortez Kennedy was chosen by the Seahawks, Keith McCants by the Buccaneers, Junior Seau by the San Diego Chargers, and Mark Carrier

Emmitt Smith had four touchdowns in a game versus the Phoenix Cardinals in his rookie season.

was selected by the Chicago Bears. And on and on they picked. But no one chose Emmitt Smith.

Suddenly, though, things began to happen: first a call from Bob Ackles, the player personnel director of the Cowboys, and not long after, a personal call from head coach Jimmy Johnson. The Cowboys *were* interested. And soon after, it was announced that Dallas had traded up and with the 17th pick selected Emmitt Smith. The Smith household erupted—and the entire neighborhood for that matter—erupted. A few hours later, Pensacola's most famous football player was in Dallas for a press conference, where he was officially welcomed into the oganization by Johnson and team owner Jerry Jones. Smith felt like he was in heaven. What 20-year-old under the same circumstances would not feel the same?

Smith finished up school, then headed for presummer camp, hanging out with two other rookies, James Washington and Vinson Smith, for the most part. They discussed how they were going to transform the Cowboys, 1-15 the year before in Johnson's first season at the helm, into winners. Of course, they knew about the bitter feelings that still existed in Dallas following Jerry Jones's unceremonial firing of legendary coach Tom Landry to make way for University of Miami coach Jimmy Johnson, but to them, that was another era and they were a part of a new one.

Smith bought himself a new car, a Datsun 300ZX, and the three tooled around town in style. By the start of summer camp in July, however, Smith was still without a contract. The sides were not even close. In late August, Smith registered at the University of Florida, not to play football but threatening to complete his senior year in the classroom.

Not until five days before the start of the season was a deal reached. Emmitt got close to $3 million for three years. Smith's response: "Bring on the NFL!"

Jimmy Johnson had other ideas, at least initially. After all, the rookie had missed all of the preseason and there were a lot of plays and formations for him to learn.

It was no suprise then that Smith's pro debut was nothing to write home about. In the season opener against the San Diego Chargers, number 22 saw spot action, gaining just 2 yards on two carries. Still, it was a thrill to be out on the same field that day wearing that helmet with the star on it among players like second-year quarterback Troy Aikman and veteran defensive end Jim Jeffcoat, representing the new and the old of the Cowboys' organization.

Late the following week, Johnson made a surprise announcement. Smith would be starting the next game against the New York Giants, a strong team that would eventually win that season's Super Bowl.

Although Emmitt started, he carried a mere six times and the Cowboys were blasted, 28–7. He did not see much more use in the next two weeks either as Dallas got off to a 1-3 start.

Finally, in the team's fifth game, against Tampa Bay, Smith took center stage. The 21-year-old rushed for 121 yards and Dallas won. The Cowboys were also buoyed by the return of receiver Michael Irvin, who had missed the first four weeks with a knee injury.

Despite his big game against the Bucs, Smith did not get the ball much the next few

If the Cowboys had beaten the Falcons in 1990, they would have been in the play-offs. But Tim Green tackled Smith in his own end zone for a safety, and Atlanta won easily, 26–7.

weeks as Dallas dropped to 3-7. From there on, though, Smith got the ball much more, and it was no coincidence that the Cowboys caught fire. Dallas reeled off wins over the Los Angeles Rams, Washington Red-skins, New Or-leans Saints, and Phoenix Cardinals to go to 7-7.

In a Thanks-giving Day win over Washington, Smith had his best game as a pro. He gained 132 yards and scored 2 touch-downs, including a season-high 48-yarder late in the game. Against the Cardinals, Smith dashed for four of his 11 touchdowns that year, capping a terrific four-game run by him and the team. And between Michael Irvin and tight end Jay Novacek, who would have a banner year catching 59 passes, and Smith's running, Aikman was able to get some breathing room, making the Cowboy passing attack much more dangerous.

Smith's—and the Cowboys'—surge got derailed in Week 15, when the Philadelphia Eagles pounded Dallas, 17–3. To make matters worse, Philadelphia's aggressive defense drilled Aikman so hard the quarterback's shoulder was separated. Yet even with backup quarterback Babe Laufenberg leading the way, the Cowboys were hoping to find a way into the playoffs the final week. But the Atlanta Falcons had other ideas and swamped Dallas, 26–7, giving the Cowboys a 7-9 record for the year.

For Smith, it was a largely positive year. He averaged just under four yards per carry and finished the season with 937 yards on the ground, plus another 228 on 24 receptions. That was the tenth highest total in the league and best among first-year players, helping to earn him NFL rookie of the year honors. He would also compete in the Pro Bowl in Hawaii.

Still, many of the goals Smith had set for himself and his team had not come true. He did not quite make the 1,000-yard mark for the season, and his team had just missed out on the playoffs. Eating at him especially was the fact that he got the ball an average of only 15 times per game. In his heart, Smith knew that he could carry 25 to 30 times and average over 100 yards a game, not just 58.

The Cowboys offense was ranked dead last that year, prompting two important postseason moves. Offensive coordinator David Shula was demoted and Norv Turner was brought on board to light a fire. This would turn out to be especially good news for one Emmitt Smith.

From the get-go, Turner made it clear that Dallas's new offense would be fairly simplified and that Smith would be a key ingredient. In Week 1 of the 1991 season, the tailback carried the ball 32 times and caught 6 passes against the Cleveland Browns. This broke team standards set by Calvin Hill and Herschel Walker for most times a Cowboys running back handled the ball in a game. Dallas won 26–24.

Smith rushed for over 100 yards (including 75 gained on a touchdown run) a week later in a 33–31 loss to Washington, and then the whole team collapsed against the Eagles, losing 24–0.

Smith had his best game as a pro the fourth week of the season, cruising for 182 yards in a 17–9 win over Phoenix. With that victory, the Cowboys turned it on, winning three more in a row over the Giants, Green Bay Packers, and Cincinnati Bengals. But they sputtered in the weeks ahead, unable to gain consistency. In one of those games, Smith lost the football deep in Oilers territory helping Houston to an overtime win. A loss to the Giants put the Cowboys at 6-5. Their playoff hopes were quickly fading away and with the undefeated Washington Redskins at RFK Stadium on tap next, it did not look very good.

But Michael Irvin caught 9 passes and Smith racked up 132 yards on a career-high 34 attempts. Not even a knee injury to Aikman in the second half (prompting backup Steve Beuerlein's insertion into the lineup), could stop the Cowboys, who won 24–21. A few days later, on Thanksgiving, Smith again went over 100 yards in a win over the Pittsburgh Steelers, putting him well into the league lead in rushing yardage.

Dallas shocked the skeptics and won its remaining games to go 11-5, with Smith finish-

Emmitt Smith jets past Martin Mayhew of Washington as the Cowboys ran past the previously undefeated Redskins in 1991.

ing the campaign with 1,563 league-leading yards. In his autobiography, Smith proudly points out, "Look at the two guys I edged: Barry Sanders and Thurman Thomas!"

And so, the Cowboys were in the playoffs as a wild card, finishing second behind Washington in the NFC East. It was the team's first winning season and first playoff season since 1985.

Jimmy Johnson, who was selected the Coach of the Year in 1990, continued to do wonders in 1991, finally putting the Tom Landry era behind him and the team.

The Cowboys drew the Mike Ditka-coached Chicago Bears in the first round at Soldier Field. Smith set the tone for a well-balanced attack by rushing for 105 yards, thus becoming the first Bear opponent to rush for over 100 yards in a postseason game since 1932.

The euphoria of it all ended a week later, though, when the Detroit Lions trounced the Cowboys, 38–6, as Smith was held to 80 yards on 15 carries. Troy Aikman, healthy again, replaced Beuerlein late in the game, to no avail. The Cowboys season ended with a thud. The Lions, meanwhile, were wiped out by the Redskins in the title game en route to the Super Bowl title.

It may have ended with a thud, but as far as the team was concerned there was plenty to celebrate. Smith and Irvin became the first two teammates to lead the league in rushing yardage and receiving yardage, respectively, and both players were named to the NFC Pro Bowl team, along with Jay Novacek and Aikman. This was the first time four offensive players on the Cowboys were chosen in the same year dating back to 1979.

The Cowboys, mired dead last a year before, had risen to the league's ninth best offensive team under Norv Turner. In the regular season, Smith averaged almost 23 carries and almost 97 yards per game to win the league title. The Cowboys have had their share of great runners over the years, from Calvin Hill to Tony Dorsett to Herschel Walker. None of them, amazingly, ever led the league in rushing.

As time would wear on, Smith's worth would become even greater. So too would his team's. From a bungling 1-15 team in 1989 to a 7-9 squad that made some noise in 1990 to a play-off unit in 1991, the Cowboys' stars had risen quickly. But this was just the beginning for the Cowboys and Smith.

5

CHAMPIONS

Before the start of the 1992 season, the Cowboys made two critical moves. First, they acquired strong safety Thomas Everett from Pittsburgh. In late August, when the Cowboys were wallowing with a sub-.500 preseason mark, they retained the services of Charles Halcy. Haley had been named the 1990 Defensive Player of the Year when he was with San Francisco. Haley reveled in his defensive end role for the Cowboys, making life very difficult for opposing quarterbacks.

The Cowboys were young that year. Awfully young. As a unit, they were the NFL's youngest team. Twenty-three players on the 47-man roster were 26 or younger. When the season started, the critics thought Dallas's youth meant that they would be lucky to finish second to Washington.

The Redskins were the Cowboys' first regular-season test. On Monday Night Football,

Emmitt Smith is about to run over Mike Singletary of the Chicago Bears—and win the NFC rushing title.

After Smith caught the winning touchdown in the fourth quarter of the 1993 NFC playoff game, Michael Irvin gave him a big hug.

Dallas blew away the defending Super Bowl champions, 23–10. Emmitt contributed his share, racking up 140 yards on the ground.

The following week, Dallas survived what started out as a blowout in its favor. Leading 34–0 against the Giants, the Cowboys wilted in windy Giants Stadium and gave up 28 straight points. They held on, though, and upped their record to 3-0, all against NFC East Division teams, when they made the Cardinals their next victim.

All of Dallas was fired up. The Cowboys themselves were enjoying their sudden status as the team to beat. With two weeks to get ready (there was a bye week in between), the hoopla reached a frenzy in the days leading up to the Cowboys' next game against the undefeated Philadelphia Eagles of Randall Cunningham, Reggie White, Keith Byars, and former Cowboy Herschel Walker.

Raucous Veterans Stadium was crazier than ever, but the Cowboys kept their composure despite an interception that set up an early Eagles touchdown. Dallas tied the game up shortly thereafter, only to go into the lockerroom at the break trailing 10–7. In the second half, Herschel Walker punished his old team. He pounded for 86 yards and scored 2 touchdowns to ignite a 21–0 run.

The Cowboys refused to let the loss get them down. "Although embarrassed and disappointed," Smith noted in his autobiography, "we all agreed with Jimmy (Johnson) after the game: There was no reason to let this crush us. The Eagles outplayed us that night. But they'd also cashed in on several of our mistakes, and we'd actually outgained them in total yardage. In the NFC East game, we'd see the Eagles again in only five weeks. This time they'd have to come to Dallas."

By their next meeting, the Dallas Cowboys, not the Philadelphia Eagles, were owners of first place.

The Cowboys went undefeated during the next few weeks, beating the Seattle Seahawks, Kansas City Chiefs, and Los Angeles Raiders. Smith broke out of a mild slump—at least by his standards—by blasting his way for 152 yards and 3 TDs against the Raiders. In the meantime the Eagles fell apart, losing three of four games.

Philadelphia still had a shot to take the conference crown, however, when the two rivals met for the second time on November 1. It was a defensive struggle for the most part. Dallas had a 3–0 lead at halftime, but relief quarterback Jim McMahon took the Eagles downfield quickly to start the third quarter. Soon after, Emmitt broke free and raced 51 yards to set up a touchdown; he scored one himself in the fourth as he gained a total of 153 yards, and Dallas put the game away, 20–10.

The good times continued the next week when Dallas whipped the Detroit Lions, 37–3, but then the lowly Rams jolted them 27–23.

Suddenly struggling, the Cowboys barely squeaked past Phoenix, 16–10. Their offense still seemed asleep halfway through their Thanksgiving Day game against the Giants. They clung to a 9–3 lead but did not look good doing it. Finally, Smith jump-started his team by grabbing a pass from Troy Aikman and crossing the goal line 26 yards later. For an encore, he jaunted 68 yards for another score. When Aikman hit Alvin Harper for another touchdown, the Cowboys could feel good about the 30–3 verdict.

It was the defense that gave the Cowboys a lift in their 13th game, a come-from-behind win over Denver in Mile High Stadium. Two interceptions led to Dallas touchdowns, but from there the game went back and forth even with Broncos quarterback John Elway sidelined. With the game clock winding down, the Cowboys turned to Emmitt with a third down and 2 at the Denver 3 yardline. The All-Pro tailback found a hole and the Cowboys had the win.

Now the 11-2 Cowboys were one victory away from clinching their first divisional title since 1985. The Redskins would not submit, nipping Dallas 20–17. But the Atlanta Falcons proved to be no such obstacle, giving up a 41–17 decision. Smith ran for 174 yards, including 132 in the second half, with a pair of touchdowns.

With the last game coming up, Emmitt Smith was in a nip-and-tuck battle with Pittsburgh's Barry Foster for the league rushing title. Earlier that Sunday, Foster finished his season with another strong outing. Smith, who had the always tough Chicago Bears to face, found himself needing 109 yards to overtake

Foster.

With Daryl "Moose" Johnston, arguably the league's best blocking fullback, and a line consisting of Nate Newton, Erik Williams, Frank Cornish, Kevin Gogan, Mark Tuinei, John Gesek, and Mark Stepnoski doing their thing, it turned out to be a day at the park for Smith.

In the third quarter, Emmitt raced 31 yards for his 18th touchdown of the season, giving the Cowboys a cushion in the game and putting

Bruce Smith tries to get the ball—or Emmitt— as Emmitt fights for yards in the 1993 Super Bowl.

himself atop the rushing leaders. By the end of the game, NFC East champion Dallas had finished off the Bears, 27–14, and Smith capped the day with 131 yards, giving him 1,713 for the year. He became the first runner to win consecutive rushing titles since Eric Dickerson turned the trick in 1983–84.

The previous year, the Cowboys were a wild-card team, meaning they had to win a preliminary game to move on in the playoffs. Now, as division champs, they were able to enjoy a week off. Soon enough, it was back to work against a familiar foe: the Eagles.

It was no contest. Dallas banged up Randall Cunningham, dropping the quarterback five times to set a rout in motion. The final score was a not-so-close 34–10. Emmitt Smith rushed for 114 yards (69 in the third quarter) and scored his first postseason touchdown, a 23-yard burst off a simple draw play. "If we go out and play the game the way we can and utilize everything we have, there is nobody that can beat us," Smith told a writer from the *New York Times*. "We have a very good team."

So did the San Francisco 49ers. The West Division champs featured Steve Young, that year's MVP, Jerry Rice, and Ricky Watters. The 49ers were the best team in the regular season, winning 14 games.

On a drizzly Sunday afternoon, January 17, 1993, the young upstarts from Dallas faced off against the veterans from San Francisco. The millions of fans watching on television and the 64,290 viewing from the Candlestick Park stands were not disappointed with this one. The scoring went back and forth in the first half. Trailing 7–3, Smith ran in for a touchdown from two yards out. The teams headed into the lockerroom knotted at 10 apiece.

Dallas took the lead in the third quarter with lengthy drives of 78 and 79 yards. Smith capped the second one with a 24-yard touchdown catch that gave Dallas a 24–13 lead. He nearly made it 31–13 early in the fourth quarter but was stopped at the 1 yardline on a fourth-down play.

Immediately, Young showed his MVP form, taking the 49ers 99 yards for a touchdown—and a 24–20 nailbiter—as 4:22 remained. Smith recalled the team's feelings at that point in his autobiography. "As we started first and 10 from our own 21, I have to admit our huddle seemed anxious. That last drive sent the momentum back to them, and if we went three and out, we knew Steve Young would have plenty of time to beat us. That's when Norv Turner made one of his gustiest calls, a first-down pass instead of a run."

The 49ers were looking for Smith to get the ball, thinking Dallas wanted to grind out some yards as the clock ticked away. Aikman stunned them by hitting Alvin Harper across the middle. Harper's defender slipped and Alvin was able to go 70 yards down to the San Francisco 9. Two plays later, Aikman again dropped back to pass, this time hitting Kelvin Martin for a 6-yard TD. When the clock hit 0:00, the scoreboard read, "Dallas 30, San Francisco 20."

The Cowboys had their sixth NFC championship, sending them to Super Bowl XXVII, their first trip to the nation's most-watched sporting event in 15 years. Pittsburgh had been their opponent back then, and it was one of the few great Super Bowls, with the Terry Bradshaw-led Steelers emerging on top, 35–31.

Buffalo's Don Beebe strips the ball away from Leon Lett. Beebe thus prevented the Cowboys from scoring their 58th and 59th points of the Super Bowl.

The 1993 Super Bowl was anything but exciting, as Dallas won their third Super Bowl with the most lopsided score in history, 52–17, over the Buffalo Bills.

It may have been a blowout, but to Smith and his teammates, the thrill of being in California for the Super Bowl was incredible. The Rose Bowl was filled to capacity—with 98,374 fans packing the ancient stadium in Pasadena, and millions more from around the country watching at home, in bars, or at restaurants. Indeed, that year's Super Bowl was viewed by more people than any other event in television history, then and now.

The game itself was a dud, even if for a short moment one might have thought otherwise. Buffalo scored first, capitalizing on a blocked punt. But from then on, it was all Dallas.

More to the point, it was all Aikman. The Cowboys signal-caller completed 22 of 30 passes for 372 yards and 4 touchdowns. Michael Irvin caught six of those passes for over 100 yards and Smith, who rushed for 108 yards (giving him over 2,000 in the 19-game season), gained another 27 on six catches.

The day was also a last hurrah for defensive coordinator Dave Wannstedt. He had announced during the previous week that he was accepting the Bears' head-coaching job, replacing the popular Mike Ditka.

The day's funniest moment came near the end of the game. Leon Lett, the big defensive lineman, grabbed backup quarterback Frank Reich's fumble and headed downfield for what looked to be a 64 yard touchdown. At the last moment, Lett slowed down and held the ball out in glee. Don Beebe, a wide receiver, was the only Bill chasing Lett, and he was able to swat the ball out of Lett's hands; it bounced out of the end zone for a Buffalo touchback.

It was the perfect ending to a laugher of a Super Bowl. The next few months would be anything but a joke to Smith, however. His contract had now expired and he was ready to make a play for big money. But team owner Jerry Jones had other ideas.

6

A MONEY BACK

Emmitt Smith and Jerry Jones had disagreed on Emmitt's value when he was first drafted. Two years later, Smith asked the team's owner to renegotiate a contract. Despite promises, Jones never followed through.

His third season complete, Smith's value had risen even more. After all, in the past two seasons he had compiled over 3,200 yards and scored 30 touchdowns while winning two straight rushing titles. And in his three seasons, he had gained 4,213 yards, putting him on the same page as some of the greatest runners in football history at that stage of their careers. He had also played in three consecutive Pro Bowls, was the first player to ever win a rushing championship and a Super Bowl title in the same season, and was the first Cowboy to run for 100 yards in the Super Bowl. In addition, in games in which he carried 20 times or more the

After the 1993 Super Bowl, owner Jerry Jones had nothing but thanks and praise for his standout runner.

Smith celebrates a touch-down in the 38–21 NFC playoff game against the San Francisco 49ers in 1994.

Cowboys were 29-1 and in games when he rushed for over 100 yards, Dallas was 21-1.

What Smith did not mention is that his ability went beyond just running the ball. By now he had become a solid receiver, another weapon for Troy Aikman. After catching 24 passes his first year, Smith followed up with 49 and 59 receptions the next two seasons, giving him another 821 yards of offense. In addition, Smith was not afraid to hit some-one, often making the block that allowed Aikman to find a receiver downfield. As a runner, Smith excelled in his ability to hold on to the ball. A Smith fumble was a rarity, indeed.

In his last year, Smith made less than $750,000 includ-ing incentives—which meant he was paid worse than many more mediocre backs. Smith felt he was worth a four-year, $17-million deal. Jerry Jones nearly choked when he heard the numbers.

Almost immediately, Jones began downplay-ing Smith's values to the Cowboys, insisting that the team could survive without him. This prompted Smith, a restricted free agent, to start testing the waters that winter.

Here was one of the best runners in history,

and amazingly there was not even a nibble. Perhaps team owners were in collusion with each other. As no other team expressed a hint of interest, Smith and his agent began to talk turkey with Jones in June. Confident that a deal could be worked out, Smith worked out with teammates during June. But it was not until early July that the Cowboys countered with their first "serious" offer. It was $9 million over four years, barely half of what Emmitt wanted.

The impasse, which started during the winter, carried over into training camp and continued into the preseason games, finally reaching into the regular season. All along, Jones preached that the Cowboys would do just fine without Smith. "Emmitt Smith is a luxury, not a necessity for the Cowboys," he said; the Cowboys "could win a Super Bowl without Emmitt Smith."

With Smith out, Derrick Lassic was given the ball in Dallas's game against Washington. Lassic also ran with the ball in the next game against Buffalo. Dallas lost both games. If ever proof was needed, this was it. The Cowboys were just not the same team without Emmitt. New York Giants lineback Corey Miller put it succinctly. "If Troy Aikman is out, his replacement can just hand Emmitt the ball and watch the options open up. But if Emmitt is out, defenses can pin their ears back and go after the quarterback. There is no one to replace Emmitt."

Only hours after the Bills game, Jones upped his offer. The two sides went back and forth a couple more times, and by week's end they came to an agreement. Smith signed a $13.6-million four-year deal. Emmitt was happy to get to play again, but the negotiations with Jones left a bitter taste in Smith's mouth.

Smith rejoined his teammates in time for their next game, at Phoenix. Lassic started and responded with a decent 14-carry, 60-yard performance. Smith got into the game late in the third quarter with Dallas already leading 17–0. He picked up 45 yards in eight runs, not bad for a guy who had not formally practiced in months. The defending Super Bowl champs won their first game of the year, 17–10.

A week later, in Dallas's home opener, Smith got his first start of 1994. Despite a slight hamstring pull, the star gained 71 yards on 13 carries, including a 22-yard touchdown dash, as Dallas romped past the Packers, 38–14.

The next week brought a rout of Indianapolis. Smith went over 100 yards for the first time, gaining 104 yards on 25 tries. Could the Cowboys become the first team to start the season 0-2 and go on to win another Super Bowl?

The Cowboys made it four in a row by knocking off the 49ers in a much-heralded showdown. It did not come easy, though, as San Francisco had a one-point lead late into the third quarter. But the Cowboys, behind Michael Irvin's 12 receptions on the day, fought back. It was a career-day for Irvin, who caught a dozen passes for 168 yards. Although Smith rushed for 92 yards and a TD, a rare fumble of his was turned into an instant touchdown for the 49ers. The 26–17 win, meanwhile, put the Cowboys in a tie with the Eagles for second place in the NFC East, a game behind New York.

In the next game, Smith had a day to remember. He lugged the ball 30 times and gained 237 yards as Dallas whipped the Eagles,

23–10. Meanwhile, the Giants were losing their game. Smith's 237-yard day set the new Cowboys standard (eclipsing Tony Dorsett's 206-yard mark) and was the best single-game performance since Waltor Payton rushed for 275 yards 16 years earlier.

Although the Cowboys rocked the Giants, 31–9, to take over first place, Aikman was knocked out of action with a hamstring pull. When it was determined that he would miss time, the Cowboys quickly signed Bernie Kosar, just released by the Cleveland Browns. Kosar played a big hand in the Cowboys' next game, against Phoenix, completing 13 of 21 passes in a 20–15 win. Dallas's seven-game winning streak, though, came to a jarring halt a week later when Atlanta stunned the Cowboys, 27–14. It was not a good game for Smith, statis-

Thomas Smith tries to prevent Emmitt Smith from scoring, but Emmitt got the touchdown anyway in the third quarter of Super Bowl XXVIII.

tically and physically, as he bruised his right quadriceps. To make matters worse for the Cowboys, the Giants won, and the two rivals were tied for first place with six weeks to go.

All week long Smith nursed his injury, and even though he was still in pain he was ready to go against Miami on Thanksgiving in what would become one of the more memorable games in Dallas history. It was a rainy, icy day in Dallas. Neither offense did much (Smith finished with a little more than 50 yards on the ground), yet the Cowboys had the lead, 14–13, with just over two minutes remaining. Miami's quarterback, Steve DeBerg, hustled the Dolphins to the Cowboy 24 in a last-ditch drive to victory. With 15 seconds left, Pete Stoyanovich's 41-yard field goal was blocked by Jimmie

Floridian Emmitt Smith models his Super Bowl ring for the Arkansas trio of Jerry Jones, President Bill Clinton, and Jimmy Johnson.

Jones. The game should have been over, but Leon Lett mistakenly went for the ball and it scooted off his foot. Instead of the play being ruled dead, it was now a live ball. The ball bounced all the way down to the 1 yardline, where the Dolphins recovered. Stoyanovich cracked the uprights for a 19-yard field goal for the win as time expired. Rather than being 8-3, the Cowboys had lost two straight and had sunk to 7-4. As December rolled in, it was do-or-die time for Dallas.

Taking advantage of an 11-day break (their next game was on a Monday night), a well-rested Dallas defeated Philadelphia. The big story was Smith. His injury woes behind him, he rushed for 172 yards to give him 409 yards against the Eagles in two games that season. Victories over the Minnesota Vikings, New York Jets, and Redskins set up a division showdown contest against the Giants in Giants Stadium on January 2.

In the win over Washington, Smith rushed for 153 yards in taking over the league rushing leadership. Just to get to that point was amazing for Smith, who missed the first two games and did not play much in the third. No runner had ever missed two games in a season and won the running crown. But Smith had managed to vault past Barry Sanders, Rodney Hampton, Barry Foster, Jerome Bettis, Thurman Thomas, and Ricky Watters.

And what a game it was in chilly Giants Stadium! The two teams hammered each other like there was no tomorrow. Smith separated his right shoulder late in the second half after a big gain, yet he finished with 168 yards on 32 carries. He also caught 10 passes for 61 yards, giving him 229 total yards while playing hurt. In overtime, Eddie Murray's 41-yard field goal won the game for Dallas, 16–13.

Smith's 168 yards gave him 1,486 for the year, good enough for his third straight rushing title, making him only the fourth runner to win three in a row. Previously, only Hall of Famers Steve Van Buren, Earl Campbell, and the superb Jim Brown turned the trick. Additionally, Smith led the league in total yards (1,900), in average yards per carry (5.3), and he became the first

Cowboy to win the league's Most Valuable Player Award. Naturally, he was picked to play in the Pro Bowl a fourth consecutive year. But there was other business to take care of first.

Two weeks after the stunning win over New York, the Cowboys played host to the Green Bay Packers in the playoffs. With Aikman finding seams through the airwaves, Dallas knocked off Green Bay, 27–17, while the 49ers were crushing the Giants, 44–3. That set up another Cowboys-49ers battle for the NFC championship. And again, it was Dallas's day to revel.

Following up on Jimmy Johnson's public prediction of a Dallas victory, the Cowboys whipped San Francisco, 38–21. Smith scored first-half touchdowns on a 5-yard run and on an 11-yard pass play, as Dallas took a 28–7 halftime lead. Early in the third quarter, the Cowboys' fortunes suddenly wavered when Aikman, who was 14 of 18 for 177 yards in the first half, left the game after being knocked cold. But Bernie Kosar kept the Cowboys breathing in the latter stages of the game. For his part, Smith gained 173 total yards (88 on the ground, 85 in the air).

For the second straight year, the Cowboys-49ers game was considered by the public as the Super Bowl game—if not in name, then in appeal. That certainly proved to be the case when the Cowboys destroyed the Bills a week later, 52–17.

Two items over the off-season raised cain for Cowboys players and fans. First, offensive coordinator Norv Turner announced that he was taking the Washington Redskins' head coaching job, and then, in March, it was announced that Jimmy Johnson was leaving, too. Jimmy

Johnson and Jerry Jones were always at odds during their reign together, and the two finally had it out during the NFL meetings in Orlando, Florida. Jimmy Johnson resigned and immediately Jerry Jones hired former Oklahoma University coach Barry Switzer. A new era was beginning in Dallas.

A new era perhaps, but to the Cowboys there was just one thing on their mind as the 1994 season got underway: threepeat. But before they could do that, they would have to contend with some problems. First, they would have to overcome the losses of four starters to free agency—guards John Gesek and Kevin Gogan, safety Thomas Everett, and linebacker Ken Norton, Jr.

Nevertheless, the Cowboys again went on to win the NFC East title with a 12-4 record, sparked, in part, by a 7-1 start. Smith's string of rushing titles came to an end as Barry Sanders outdistanced him, 1,883 yards to 1,484. For the first time in his pro career, an injury actually kept Smith on the sidelines. In the 15th week of the campaign, he injured his left hamstring in a game against New Orleans. While he probably could have played against the Giants the last week had it been a crucial game, it was decided to rest Smith for the playoffs.

Smith was back for the first playoff game, versus Green Bay, but not for long. He aggravated his hamstring on his seventh carry of the game, and his day was over just a short time before the end of the first quarter. By then, the Cowboys were in control and on their way to a convincing 35–9 win. Smith had scored a touchdown on the first Cowboys drive and the team as a whole had gained 191 yards. In the first half, Aikman and Harper teamed up for a 94-

Lawrence Taylor and actress Rosie Perez congratulate Emmitt Smith for winning the Pro Football Player of the Year title at the 1994 Espy Awards.

yard TD play, the longest in NFL postseason history.

The pressing question heading into the NFC finale in San Francisco was whether Smith would be OK for the game. He was, but the Cowboys were not. Taking advantage of three first-quarter turnovers, the 49ers bolted to a 21–0 lead within seven minutes and coasted from there, 38–28.

The Cowboys made it back to the Super Bowl the following season and beat the Pittsburgh Steelers, 27-17. Along the way, Smith won the league's rushing title with 1,773 yards.

"Down the road I'd like to make the Hall of Fame, and also the Dallas Cowboys' Ring of Honor. And I hope to surpass Walter Payton's career rushing record of 16,726 yards", says Smith, who has proven that hard work can pay off in a big way. No matter where he goes from here, Emmitt Smith, number 22, is already among the greatest running backs in NFL history.

CHRONOLOGY

1969   Emmitt Smith born in Pensacola, Florida, on May 15

1987   Announces his intention to attend the University of Florida; in his freshman year, he leads the SEC in rushing

1990   Picked by the Dallas Cowboys in the first round of the NFL draft; rushes for personal best 4 touchdowns in a game versus the Phoenix Cardinals; named rookie of the year

1991   Leads league in rushing

1992   Leads league in rushing; has a career-high 12 receptions in a game versus the Phoenix Cardinals

1993   Helps lead team to Super Bowl victory 52–17 over Buffalo Bills; runs for a career-high 237 yards in a game versus Philadelphia Eagles; leads league for third year straight in rushing

1994   Named NFL most valuable player for 1993 season; again leads Cowboys to a 30–12 win over Buffalo Bills in Super Bowl; named most valuable player of the Super Bowl

1995   Wins fourth NFL rushing title with 1,773 yards. Becomes the only player in NFL history to rush for at least 1,400 yards in 5 consecutive seasons

1996   Captures third place on the NFL's all-time list for scoring 108 career TD's

STATISTICS

EMMITT SMITH

YEAR	RUSHING				RECEIVING			
	NO	YDS	AVG	TD	NO	YDS	AVG	TD
1990	241	937	3.9	11	24	228	9.5	0
1991	365	**1563**	4.3	12	49	258	5.3	1
1992	373	**1713**	4.6	18	59	335	5.7	1
1993	283	**1486**	5.3	9	57	414	7.3	1
1994	368	1484	4.0	21	50	341	6.8	1
1995	377	1773	4.7	25	62	375	6.0	0
1996	327	1204	3.7	12	47	249	5.3	3
TOTALS	2,334	10,160	4.3	108	348	2,200	6.5	7

POST-SEASON PLAY

YEAR	NO	YDS	AVG	TD	NO	YDS	AVG	TD
1991	41	185	4.5	1	1	2	2.0	0
1992	71	336	4.7	3	13	86	6.6	1
1993	66	280	4.2	3	13	138	10.6	1
1994	27	118	4.4	3	4	8	2.0	0
1995	74	298	4.0	6	6	60	10.0	0
1996	39	196	5.0	2	7	24	3.4	0

bold indicates league-leading statistics

SUGGESTIONS FOR FURTHER READING

Fisher, Mike. *The Boys are Back: The Return of the Dallas Cowboys.* New York: Summit Books, 1993.

Shapiro, Leonard. *The Dallas Cowboys.* New York: St. Martin's Press, 1993.

Smith, Emmitt, with Steve Delsohn. *The Emmitt Zone.* New York: Crown Publishers, 1994.

ABOUT THE AUTHOR

Dan Hirshberg is the editor of the *Star-Gazette* in Hackettstown, New Jersey, and is the author of *Phil Rizzuto: A Yankee Tradition.* He lives in Hackettstown with his wife, Susan, and two children, Nathan and Melanie.

INDEX